GOD SEES,
GOD KNOWS
and GOD
DELIVERS

GOD SEES, GOD KNOWS *and* GOD DELIVERS

LORETTA THOMAS

XULON PRESS

Xulon Press
2301 Lucien Way #415
Maitland, FL 32751
407.339.4217
www.xulonpress.com

Paperback ISBN-13: 978-1-66284-587-1
Ebook ISBN-13: 978-1-66284-588-8

DEDICATION

To my parents, James and Emma Robertson, whom I love and miss! You were always there for me. May you both rest in peace, until we meet again.

To my children: Kim, Charles, Carla, and Roxanne

I thank the Lord for blessing me with each one of you. I know growing up was not a joy. As a matter of fact, we were probably one of the most dysfunctional families God has ever seen. No, I'm only kidding. Throughout the Bible, there were many dysfunctional families. It all started with Adam and Eve's disobedience. Cain killed his brother, Abel. Joseph was thrown into a hole to die by his own brothers, and then sold, etc. I love you all very much. I do believe what the enemy meant for evil, God is going to turn it around for His good. As your father and I found out (the hard way), Jesus is the only Way. Jesus went through a gruesome death for each of us. It takes each of us to find Him for ourselves. He stands with His arms wide open, waiting. The Bible says, "He stands at the door and knocks," (Rev. 3:20). This means He is knocking on your hearts. It's up to each of you to let Him in. His love is real! Without Him, we are nothing and can do nothing right.

I pray that you will look past the embarrassing part(s) and see how the Lord has delivered me from my past behavior. My prayer is that this book will be an eye-opener for each of you, and all that read it.

Love, Mom!

ACKNOWLEDGEMENTS

First and foremost, I want to thank my Heavenly Father for His love for me! I thank Him for knowing my heart and delivering me. God has truly been with me during the writing of this book. The struggle has been real ever since I put it in my mind to finish this book. When I felt discouraged, God showed up in ways unimaginable. He is so awesome! When I was having problems with my computer, God sent me a hawk that came and sat on the post on our deck. Hawks represent determination, focus, leadership, clarity, future planning, etc.

It happened again, only three weeks before getting this book sent to the producer. I lost my "Introduction." It literally vanished, (so I thought)! I also couldn't get into my Microsoft software, due to switching over from my tablet to my laptop. I couldn't remember my password and signed in with the wrong email. Again, I got discouraged, and the hawk showed up! The next time, the hawk flew onto the top of the umbrella on the deck, where I could see him outside the glass door. I tell you this to say God is so amazing. The message I received was to stay focused and be determined. To God be the glory!

I acknowledge and thank the following people for their encouragement and prayers: my sisters, Pearl Robertson and Debbie Robertson; my niece Deborah Jones, my friends/sisters in the Lord, Sheriel Brown and Annette Stevens; my North Carolina friend and sister(s) in the Lord, Mary Witcher and her daughter, Monikka Wright, who insisted and encouraged me to continue writing this book after I testified at their church one year, and Pastor Dwayne Barnes and Mary Grace Barnes.

My thanks also goes to, my great nephew and his wife, Bryan and Sonia Jones, for making it possible to publish this book.

TABLE OF CONTENTS

INTRODUCTION

We have all been born into sin because of Adam and Eve's disobedience. Today, there are so many people who are struggling in one way or another. It could be from physical or mental illness, abandonment, low self-esteem, P.T.S.D., A.D.H.D., domestic violence, rape, sickness, loneliness, you name it.

The main reason for this book is to bring hope to those who are suffering in one way or another. There is no problem or situation too hard for God. *"Behold, I am the Lord, the Lord of all flesh; is there anything too hard for Me?"* (Jer. 32:27). God is our Creator. He made us and knows all about us, from the day we were born until this very moment. He sees what you have gone through and what you are going through. He loves us so much, that He has made a way of escape from any situation. *"For God so loved the world that He gave His only begotten Son, that whoever believes in Him should not perish but have everlasting life,"* (John 3:16). All one has to do is believe and receive Jesus Christ in their life and He will make all things new. *"Therefore, if anyone is in Christ, he is a new creation; old things pass away; behold, all things become new,"* (2 Cor. 5:17).

The gift of salvation is yours; all you need to do is receive it.

CHAPTER 1

FAMILY LIFE

*I*t all started whenI lived on Diamond Street, Providence, RI, when I was born. At a young age, maybe two or three years old, one of the memories I had was when my brother got hit by a car. Thank God he didn't get badly injured; I think he had a broken arm. I remember that we had to hide and be quiet, because my grandmother said the gypsies were coming near our house. She told me that gypsies steal children. My siblings and I would duck down away from the window. My dad's sister lived in a house in front of ours, and his brother lived at the other end of the street.

At Christmas time, we would always wake up before our parents, but we would have to check with them before we could open our gifts. Our eyes would always light up when we saw the gifts under the tree. We children never knew we were poor; we loved whatever gifts we received. One year I got a tall white doll with brown hair, and my older sister got one with blonde hair. She decided to give my doll a haircut. I wasn't very happy with that haircut; it was a mess. One Christmas, she got a ballerina doll, and I was jealous. I got a typewriter, which I loved. The boys got train sets and cars, etc. We also got new clothes, so we were happy! There were only four of us children at that time.

Our next move was to Blackstone Street. At that house, I got chickens and/or bunny rabbits for Easter. One day, we got our first dog, a German Shepard. I don't really remember his name. I don't even know what happened to him. I don't think he lived very long either. I remember us digging a hole and burying him in the backyard.

One night, the neighbors downstairs told my parents that the house was on fire. It was the middle of the night. My parents woke us up. As they were rushing us out of the house, they almost forgot our baby brother. The house was burning with large flames, as we stood outside in our pajamas on that cold winter night. People were wrapping blankets around us as we watched the firefighters trying to put the fire out. The house was a total loss. We spent the rest of the night at our Nana Shepard's house. Due to our home being a total loss, we ended up moving in with my nana (my mom's mother). My mom's two sisters and a brother also lived there.

So it was the six of us and the four of them; let's say it was kind of crowded. Even though it was crowded, we were a happy family. I slept on mattresses on the floor. There were mice there also. I'm not sure how long we stayed there. My parents were able to purchase a house on Pavilion Avenue, which became our next home.

As the movers (family members I'm sure) moved things into the new house, we had to stay out of the way. We sat on the floor in front of our the black and white T.V. Mom was putting things in their proper place. I watched the *Ed Sullivan Show, Howdy Doody, Captain Kangaroo, Bozo the Clown, Casper the Friendly Ghost, Porky Pig,* Shirley Temple, and many more shows and cartoons on that T.V.

The house on Pavilion Avenue is where I grew up. I went to elementary school, middle school and high school there. That was home! In that home, came two more siblings: a baby brother, Danny, and a baby sister, Debbie, making a total of six children in all. My father was in the Army, I guess I was too young to remember. My oldest sister, Pearl, is four years older than me; my oldest brother, Sonny, is fourteen months older than me, and my brother, Bobby, (who passed away in 2015) was twenty months younger than me. Let's just say we were close in age, "stair steps," as they called children back in that day.

My nana, two aunts, and uncle moved in up on the second floor. I enjoyed them living upstairs. I was always visiting and eating upstairs with them. I always would spend time with my aunt Elaine, she was about eight years older than me. She loved to sing and dance, and always bought clothes and shoes. I also enjoyed my uncle Bud. He worked for the Providence Journal. I would dye his hair and go get his cigarettes from the store. My oldest aunt, Muriel, got married the same day that my youngest sister was born. Her husband, Uncle Dennis, was in the army and was stationed in Massachusetts, where they lived.

My father worked two to three jobs after he got out of the army, to make ends meet. He would come home, eat, and go off to another job. He was a very dedicated father; he made sure we had food on the table and clothes on our backs, even though I had to wear some hand-me-downs. My dad may have worked two or three jobs, but when Sunday came, we were in church. I don't know how he managed to do that working that many jobs. It seemed like every time the church doors were open, we were there. We belonged to the Ebenezer Baptist Church, in Providence, RI.

My dad came from a family that enjoyed music and singing. He, his sister, three brothers, and brother-in-law, had a singing group. We children also had a singing group, called "The Robertson Singers," which consisted of my three siblings, myself, and five to six cousins. We would have rehearsal at different homes and sing at different church functions. I sang soprano and lead most of the songs. I was always nervous singing in front of crowds, but God brought me through. The congregation would shout, "Sing, children!" That made us sing even better.

Our teen years got rough. My brother, Sonny, and my brother, Bobby, always seemed to get into trouble. It seemed like if my father wasn't at work, he was fussing about something or at someone. I felt that he was unfair. He blamed us for things we didn't do. If someone did something and didn't own up to it, we'd all get in trouble. My sister told me we all got whippings, but I don't ever remember getting a whipping. Dad would never listen to us; he would jump to conclusions. My brothers would really get beatings. Dad would take them down to the basement. I remember crying when my younger brother, Bobby, was getting a beat down. It sounded like he was being killed. My mother would yell at my father to stop; sometimes he would, but it sometimes seemed to last forever. Eventually, both brothers, Sonny and Bobby, came of age, left, and never came back. My oldest sister started doing her own thing, and ended up moving to D.C. with two of our great aunts. She has her own story to tell!

When I was about six years old, I got hit by a car. I was going to mail a letter for a neighbor. I thank God that the car didn't run me over, but it knocked me down. They say if the car had rolled one more time, I would have been badly injured or died. I got up and tried to run home, but was stopped by someone who saw the accident. I was forced to sit in a chair in front of a lady's house. Someone went and got my mother. We went in the ambulance to the hospital. I did have a concussion, and was bruised.

CHAPTER 2

LIFE BEGAN

School Days

I was out of school, I guess for a week. It was time for me to go into the first grade. I had learning problems. The teachers wanted to put me in the un-graded room, now known as Special Ed. My mother stood up for me and wouldn't let them put me in that class. I did repeat the first grade. I also had to go to speech class at another school, but I survived elementary school!

Then there was middle school. I felt humiliated most of the time, especially when I had to read out loud. I hated reading. I was a slow reader and didn't really comprehend what I read. One day, (the only day I remember) I had to stand in front of the class and give a book report. I'm not even sure of my grade, but I know how I felt standing in front of the class. That day, I was even having a bad hair day. For some reason, I wore my hair out. It was a very humid day and my hair looked like a bush or a wild afro. My face felt like it was on fire. I was so humiliated!

Then there was high school. On the first day, I did not know where to go. I thank God I found a friend, Judy, who seemed to have most of the same classes as I had. We remained friends throughout our high school years, and are friends to this day. My friend started dating one of the guys in our high school. I had guys who liked me, but I was not interested in them.

My Dating Days

My dating possibly started when I was in the twelfth grade. I went out with my cousin's cousin (on her mother's side). I went out with him a short span of time. I really wasn't interested in him. There were guys at church that liked me also, but I didn't really like any of them. I did kind of like one guy, but he was silly. I was wrong about that one. My mistake! He ended up being very educated. He and his wife are now pastors of a church. There was another guy who I went out with and I enjoyed. I ended up being unfaithful to him, as he was on his way to serve in the Navy. He wanted to marry me, even after I apologized, but I just couldn't. I ended our relationship. I knew that I hurt him and his family. I truly was sorry. I thank God he found a good wife and has a beautiful family now!

There was this other guy that was also at our church. He was friends with my brother, and his sister was friends with my sister. He had always tried to go out with me, but I knew he was a player. I didn't know why, but I gave in and went out with him, maybe a couple of times. Well, one night I really gave into him, and he got what he wanted. I fell for his line. I guess I really thought he cared for me. After that night, that was the last I saw or heard from him. He joined the service and moved on. From that night on, I fell into Satan's trap for sure.

Satan's Trap

I started sleeping with different guys. Some guys I knew, and some I didn't know. I was looking for love in the way of sex. I ended up sleeping with one guy who I believed drugged me at a club. Somehow, I ended up in the bed with him, and when I woke up, he was gone. I'm not sure how I got there or how I got home. I do know that I was infected with a sexual disease called herpes simplex virus. One day, I got a rash on my right leg, that was similar to a cold sore. Unfortunately, it would be gone for years, and show up when I least expected. It left a dark mark on my leg. It took me years to realize where it came from, but God revealed it to me while writing this book. Sin is sin, is sin! God is a just God; He must punish sin. Somethings we bring onto ourselves. God is also a forgiving God. "If we confess our sins, He is faithful and just to forgive us of our sins to cleanse us from all wickedness." (1 John 1:9) I believed God for complete healing, in Jesus's name.

More Than a Kiss

My friend, Teresa (name changed), was going to have a New Year's Eve party, so we started inviting people. The brother of our church's pastor, who was in the military, was visiting for a week or two, so we invited him. It started out being an okay party, which was held in the basement of Teresa's mother's house. The party was okayed by her mother. There ended up being alcohol at the party, and I found myself spending a lot of time with the pastor's brother. We had a New Year's Eve kiss. We ended up going out, maybe the following weekend. I wasn't sure how I got my father to let me take his car. I probably lied and said I was going to my cousin's house. I picked up John (name changed) and we went and parked in the park.

Well, I must not have realized that it was as late as it was. My father sent the police looking for me once he found out that I didn't go to my cousins. There was a knock on the window of the car. It was a policeman standing outside the window. It was embarrassing since we were engaged in making out. The officer said, "Your father said to get home." I had to drive John back to his brother's, my pastor's house. When I got home, I didn't know what to expect. My father was angry, but I didn't get knocked out. He let me know that if I got pregnant, they would put me away. Well, I did get pregnant by my pastor's brother. As I mentioned, he was only visiting for a week or two. So, by the time I found out that I was pregnant, he was long gone. I don't even remember us communicating after the one night we spent alone, not even about a baby on the way. Maybe we did, but I didn't remember.

Once my parents and I found out, it became a living nightmare. I had to go to the pastor's house and apologize to him and his wife for my fornication with his brother, and to give them the news of my being pregnant. Not only about being pregnant, but about who the father was. I had to stand before the church and tell them that I had sinned and that I was pregnant. How embarrassing! The Bible tells me, "All have sinned and come short of the glory of God," (Rom. 3:23). They all sinned in some way or another and didn't confess their wrongdoings in front of the church. Because my sin was about to grow bigger over nine months, everyone would see and possibly know who the father was. Not to mention who the grandparents would be!

CHAPTER 3

GOD KNOWS BEST

I had a couple of baby showers, one from my job and one from my family and friends. One day, I could not feel the baby move, so my parents took me to the hospital. I was nine months pregnant at the time. I was admitted and went straight into the delivery room, where I didn't remember anything. I did remember was coming out, and my parents were standing over me while I was being rolled into my room, saying, "God knows best," and I knew then, that the baby had died. I was told that he was stillborn, meaning that the umbilical cord had wrapped around his neck. I was so sad; that hurt so much! I had to lay in the hospital bed while other mothers got their babies for feeding. I cried so much. The men from the funeral parlor came next. They gave their condolences, and asked me if it was ok to bury the baby in a shoebox. Really, a shoebox? All I could say was yes; I knew my baby was with Jesus. I also knew my father wasn't paying for anything else. I never got to see my baby boy, but I know I will meet him someday.

When I went home from the hospital, I didn't remember having any conversation about the baby. I'm not sure if I blocked it out and everyone else blocked it out also. I never asked any questions. I can't even remember where all the gifts went. I think I gave them away to two of my cousins who were expecting. Both had baby boys. One named her son Mark, who became my godson, and the other named her son Kevin, which was one of the names I think I had picked for my baby. The other name I picked was Keith. I guessed that the father, the pastor, and his wife were glad that the baby didn't make it. I know that I will see my son when I leave this body and unite with him in glory.

CHAPTER 4
THOSE DARN DRESS BLUES

One day, I went to my friend's house. Her mother had visitors. There were four or five marines visiting her. These guys were much younger than her mother. They were my age. Well, my friend and I found that we both had one we were interested in. I ended up talking to one who I wasn't really looking at, and she ended up talking to another one. They all looked good in their dress blues! I ended up dating the one who liked me; I guess I liked him also. We would talk almost all night on the house's landline telephone (no cellphones back then). One night, my dad was telling me to get off the phone and go to bed. It was probably one o'clock or so in the morning. I would reluctantly get off and go up to my room. I found my boyfriend was saying all the right things, and my dad was getting on my last nerve. I shared that with my boyfriend and he asked me to marry him. I said yes.

I broke the news to my parents and knew right away that they didn't approve. They had already met him. My mind was made up, and I became engaged. Charles had told me that he was going to be transferred to California, a place where I always wanted to go. We wasted no time in making plans for the wedding. I spoke to the residing pastor of the church at that time and planned our small wedding. It would only be family and a few of my friends. We got married that next month, which was August. To tell you the truth, I didn't really know that much about Charles. I found out that he smoked marijuana the night of our wedding, at a party given to us by my maid of honor. He, his best man, (who was one of the marines from my friend's mother's house) and some other guys were in the bedroom smoking, along with my maid of honor's brother. That was a shock! What had I gotten myself into? Good question, but it came too late.

We ended up moving in with my brother and his wife for a short time, until our apartment became available. I learned a lot more about my husband really fast. I learned that my husband had joined the Marines right after graduating from high school. He was sent to Vietnam after boot camp. When I met him, he had come back to the United States for a short time. He was stationed in Quonset Point, Rhode Island. I also found out that he was the second oldest of fourteen children. I now had four brothers-in-law and eight sisters-in-law, since one of his sisters had passed.

Out of the Frying Pan and Into the Fire

I also found out that my husband liked to go out and leave me home alone. He came home late one night, and I must have been upset and said something to him about it. Well, he hit me and I saw stars. He slapped me around, as if I had done something wrong. Well, that would have been a good time to get out of that marriage, but I heard the words my aunt said, "That marriage won't last." I was sure my dad felt the same way. I believed that played a large part of my answer, "Why?" The next day, when we went to visit my parents, I acted like I got my black eye accidently from his elbow. And the story goes on. I was very naïve, or as my dad used to say, fickle.

Within nine months, our first child, Kim, was born on May 24, 1971. In February of 1972, my husband was transferred to California. Now I was about to move 3,000 miles away from home. My mother was sad to see us leave; I knew my mother knew what kind of marriage I was in. My daughter Kim was nine months old when I became pregnant with our second child. On our way to California, we stopped at his parent's home in Louisiana, where my husband was originally from. I met just about the whole family. Most of his siblings were living at home still. His oldest brother and one of his sisters had moved already, which meant ten children were still living in a three-bedroom, one bathroom home. Our kids had to take baths in someone else's bathwater, as did their aunts and uncles. The parents raised chickens, which ran around the house. They also raised hogs, which they kept at another location. They would go and feed them until they got a certain size. My mother-in-law had a garden in the backyard with all kinds of vegetables. She also worked out of the home, cleaning homes. Charles's father worked at the Ford company. After work, he would sit on the back porch, smoke his cigarettes, and drink his strong coffee.

CHAPTER 5
LIFE IN CALIFORNIA

From Louisiana, we started our journey to California. My son was born on September 20, 1972. My life in California wasn't easy. I continued getting beatings for no reason. His guilt played a part in my beatings. My husband had me smoke marijuana right along with him. I thank God that He always kept an eye on my children and kept them safe. I don't remember smoking in front of them. I also thank Him that I never really got high from the marijuana. One night, he brought angel dust home. I may have had a buzz, but it didn't affect me like it did him. I'll never forget that night. Charles got so high that he wanted to get in his car and end his life. I literally sat on him on the floor and prayed to God to keep his mind from doing anything stupid. He really could have knocked me off of him. I only weighed about 100 pounds, but he weighed around 165 pounds. It really was not God's desire for him to commit suicide that night. He was wasted! God was truly there with us. I always thanked God for keeping my children safe from any danger or harm.

One time, my oldest daughter, Kim, and three other toddlers decided to walk around the apartment complex. We lived in an apartment with other military families, but not on the base. I was not sure why I, or no one else, was looking after these children. We ended up walking the whole complex looking for them, and I think we also called the police. Thank God, someone found them and brought them back. That was scary! Thank God, He kept them safe.

One time (well, more than one time), my husband got mad at me for something and started beating me. I ran out of the house to a neighbor's house; I would hide in their closet. I was so afraid that he would come looking for me. The neighbor(s) called the police. The police came and questioned me and him. They told him to go cool off. I went back to the house with the kids. This happened more than I could remember. He would cool off and things would be okay, until the next time. I always forgave him. Let me say that again: I always forgave him. *Why?*

We purchased our first house through the V.A. I hate to think of the memories of living in that house. Some things I have blocked out, or wish not to remember. I do know one thing for sure: I was one stressed mother/wife. I smoked cigarettes like crazy. I would be cleaning in one room, lay my cigarette down, and go into another room and light up another cigarette. I thank God we never had a fire. My parents came to visit us. The look on their faces, especially my mother's face, scared me. I was so thin; I probably looked anorexic. I was around twenty-eight years old at that time. After they left, I made a doctor's appointment and found out that I was only ninety-eight pounds. That really scared me!

The day came when Charles was being sent to Okinawa. He decided to take us back to Rhode Island to stay with my family while he was away. Hallelujah! I was pregnant with our third child. I really enjoyed being home with my family. It was such a peaceful atmosphere! My younger sister, Debbie, was grown now, and we enjoyed each other's company. I shared a lot of things with her. Then came the birth of our new baby girl, Carla. Carla was born on September 13, 1974. Debbie and I named her.

My husband and I would write to each other. I let him know when the baby was born. Carla was about a year old when my husband came back from Okinawa. All that I went through while I was in California, and I still went back with him. Really? Another *Why?*

Once back in California, we purchased our second home. Our fourth child was born on November 1, 1976, our third little girl, Roxanne. I was truly a full-time mother, caring for four small children, with a husband who was in the marines, and I was 3,000 miles away from my mother and family. The time came for my husband to decide to stay in the marines or get out of it. I told him that if he didn't get out of the service, I was going to leave him. Where did that boldness come from? Surprisingly, I didn't get beat up for saying that either. I think he was ready to get out, so he could really do his own thing. I believed he was ready to be free from the service. He served a total of eleven years. At this time, he was even a Drill Instructor for the last one or two years of his service.

That brings me to a night that I remember very clearly. After talking to him on the phone, I knew he was tired and had had a hard day. I gave the kids a bath and put their dad's white t-shirts on them. I didn't know why, but that's what I put on them. The baby was big enough to stand up in her crib, and the other children were playing in the room. I told them to stay in the room and play. I felt the need to spend time with Charles. We were eating, watching television, smoking marijuana, and drinking wine. It seemed like I always was trying to please him. I heard the children crying, so I said, "Let me go check to see what's wrong." When I went into their bedroom, I took the baby out of the crib. As I was walking into my bedroom and talking to the other kids, I noticed that the t-shirts they were wearing were illuminated. They were as bright as a light that was turned on at nighttime. I felt the presence of God in that room. I remember thanking the Lord for being there with my children, and knowing that He knew my heart. He knew that I was being torn between them, my husband, and Him. I wanted to do the right thing. I wanted to be a good mother and a good wife. I realized I was making my husband my god. I was pleasing him and not God. I said a small prayer and I talked with the kids, and they went back to playing. I went back to be with my husband. That was truly an eye-opening experience for me.

The Cry of Forgiveness

One night after that, when my husband didn't come home for a few nights (as usual). In the middle of the night, I *cried out to the Lord to forgive me of my sins, and to deliver me from all evil.* I called on Jesus to save me. I wanted out of that situation. I was tired of living with a man who did not care about me or our children, a man who didn't care enough to come home and be a father and husband. I knew there were other women in his life, along with the drugs. I had had enough! I knew that Jesus was the only answer. That night, I asked Jesus to forgive me of my sins (all the sins), including the sins of my past. I asked Him to forgive me of sins known and unknown. I asked Him to cleanse me from all unrighteousness and to save me. I felt the presence of the Lord in that room, and I started singing to the glory of God. All those old songs that I had used to sing when I was a child came back to me. I sang "Jesus Loves Me, This I Know, for The Bible Tells Me So," "Nobody Knows the Trouble I See; Nobody Knows but Jesus," "I Come to The Garden Alone," and "I Want to be Ready." I was so in the presence of the Lord!

Here is where I have to give credit to my father, God rest his soul. My father was faithful in taking us children to church; I learned as a child growing up, that if I called on the name of Jesus, I would be saved. Jesus died for sinners, and I truly was <u>a</u> sinner. I knew if I called Him, that He would answer me. He would help me. He loved me; He cared for my children and me. I started going to church with a neighbor. The kids even went to vacation Bible school. They learned a song, which I had to help them with: "I will make you fishers of men, if you follow Me." I started attending the ladies' Bible study on Monday nights.

A new year was coming with 1979, and I asked Charles to go to church with me on New Year's Eve. To my surprise, he did go. He also went out when we got back from church. I went in front of the church when the altar call was made. I wanted to publicly show that I had decided to follow Jesus. I continued to go to the ladies' Bible studies. I received a scripture that spoke to me, and I can truly say that that scripture helped me get delivered from that situation. It said, "Open thou my eyes, that I may behold wondrous things out of thy law," (Ps. 119:18). I prayed that scripture every time I prayed.

My Eyes Were Opened

One night, we had to use candles in the house. The electricity was turned off. Charles hadn't paid the bill. My husband had a good job at the Post Office. It got to a place where, not only was he doing drugs, he was also dealing drugs. He was not bringing money home from his job. That night when he was getting ready to go to work, I had to light candles in the bedroom. When he left, I remember blowing out the candles and I got on my knees to pray. While praying, I prayed my favorite scripture at that time: "Open thou my eyes, that I may behold wondrous things out of thy law." Evidently, I fell asleep on my knees. When I woke up, I was startled. The candle was lit and glowing. I knew that I had blown it out before I knelt down to pray. At that moment, I felt the presence of the Lord in the room. I started praising Him and giving Him the glory. I knew that I was going to be set free from that situation. God had heard my heart's cry. There was another scripture that I also prayed: "Thy Word is a Lamp unto my feet and a light unto my path," (Ps. 119:105).

Christmas Eve came, and we had no gifts for the kids. That was a time when Charles had been gone for days. When he did come home, late, of course, that Christmas Eve, he didn't have any gifts, or money to buy gifts for the kids. He had to go borrow money, and went to a drug store just before they closed and got toys . That was sad, so sad!

I started 1979 off by trusting in the Lord and knowing that He was going to work things out. The pastor of the church I was attending gave me the name of a lawyer. At this time, I had a job, trying to make ends meet. The kids had a babysitter. When I went to work on Friday, I left early to see the lawyer and explained my situation to him. I let him know that I was a battered wife. He told me that my husband would get served the divorce papers on Monday, and that I should let my husband know he was going to be served with divorce papers. Right! Had he not heard me? *Hello,* I was a battered wife!

CHAPTER 6

FEAR VS. FAITH

I had the whole weekend to get my nerve up to tell my husband, but I couldn't. When I asked the pastor to pray for me, he was flirting with me. *Really*? I never mentioned it to the women's group, or anyone, for that matter.

Monday morning came, and I used Charles's car (which was his love) to take the three kids to school. I could not bring myself to go back to the house. I had Roxanne with me; she was two years old at the time. I drove around for hours. I knew my husband was furious by this time, not knowing where I was. He usually slept most of the morning after working at nights. Now, it was in the evening. The kids were home from school. They usually walked home. I was really afraid, not knowing if he got served with those papers or not. I kept driving in circles. I never went anywhere by myself in his car. I didn't really know San Diego like that. I ended up running out of gas near a friend's house. I remembered that area, thank God.

I went to a payphone and called my friend. I explained to her what I had done. She told me to go to her house, that the kids should be home from school, and that she would be there shortly. Not only was she home shortly after, but so was her husband, who was a friend of my husband, from the Marines. Well, shortly after they got home, the telephone rang, and it was my husband on the other end. I reluctantly spoke to him and explained to him that I ran out of gas because I was afraid to come home. He said he wasn't going to do anything, (yeah right!) and for me to come home. He wanted me to borrow some money for gas and food. Well, what else was I going to do? The other kids were home from school and they needed me. So, I did as he said. I borrowed money, got gas, and went to the market to get food for the kids.

When I got home and put the groceries on the counter, I immediately got slapped around. Not only for being gone all day, but evidently, the pastor had called several times asking for me. The kids were standing there in the kitchen. He made them go into their room. His brother was there at the time and never said anything to help me. As a matter of fact, he left. I was forced into our bedroom, where I was beaten, with a capital "B." I was punched, knocked to the floor, kicked, slapped, and even cut with a pocket knife. All I could think of was that Jesus went through worse than this for me. I didn't know if I was going to die that night or not. I heard the doorbell ring and a loud knock on the door. He had me go into our bathroom. He closed both the bathroom and bedroom doors. He told me not to come out. I heard him talking. I heard the Holy Spirit say, "Go." I went and stood outside the bedroom door. The living room door was right there. I remember seeing my children's babysitter. Her facial expression said it all. He realized I had come out of the room. He slammed the door in her face.

Now angrier than before, he made me go back into the bedroom. The beating started all over again. He ran hot water in the sink and he was going to put my face in it. I already was petrified of water. This time, he made me snort cocaine (which I never knew was in our home). I could see the devil in his red eyes and I held my arms out (as Jesus did on the cross) and cried, "Jesus, Jesus, Jesus." The doorbell rang again. He put me back in the bathroom and said don't come out. Again, the Holy Spirit told me, "Go."

This time, I saw two police officers. He tried to close the door on them, but couldn't. I walked out that front door praising God. I was free from that situation. Before I knew it, he had closed the door and

I screamed, "My four children are in there!" Unfortunately, it was two police women that came to the house. They immediately called for backup. By the time the SWAT team got there, helicopter and all, my husband had jumped over a six foot fence with all four children. The officers had put me into the police car in the backseat, and kept asking me questions. I felt like I did something wrong; I felt like the criminal. All I could do was pray for my children, and praise God because I was alive and free, but very concerned now for my children.

I thank God that He kept my kids safe. I thank God Charles did not have a mind to hurt them. I was taken to a nearby hospital, but was never looked at by a doctor, because I didn't have any insurance information on me. I had my picture taken by the police, who continued to question me. They told me that I was luckier (blessed) than the other lady who had just come in. I praised the Lord for keeping me through it all. The nurse asked me if I wanted to have the chaplain come in and speak to me, and I said yes. I believe he was Catholic. All I could do was praise the Lord and pray for the safety of my children, which I was sure he probably did also. I didn't really know how bad I was hurt. I didn't feel any pain, probably due to the cocaine. I told God that if He let me live, I would tell other women of His goodness, and that He was the only way.

After laying there for I don't know how long, I was able to call the president of the ladies' Bible study. She came and got me, and brought me to Kaiser E.R., where I did have insurance. I was examined there. Thank God, I didn't have any broken bones, but believe me, I was truly bruised from head to toe. I was given pain/sleeping pills, even though I didn't have any pain at the time. My friend took me home with her. She had told me that she and her family would probably be gone in the morning to school and to work, but I was welcome to feel at home. She lived close to my home. I had told her that I was going to call my sister-in-law in Los Angeles to come and get me. I did take a sleeping pill, so I could sleep. When I woke up, as she said, they had all gone. When I tried to stand up, I immediately fell to the floor, due to the medicine being so powerful, and probably because I hadn't eaten in days. I crawled to the phone, which was up on the wall. Finally, I reached for the phone and called my sister-in-law, Eloise. She and her husband did come to get me that evening. She couldn't believe what she saw. I really looked terrible. I stayed with her until the following Monday, and then made my way back to San Diego, so that I could press charges. I still didn't know the whereabouts of my children. When I went back to San Diego (by bus), my eyes were truly spiritually opened to the lost people. I saw homeless people, troubled faces, and hurting people. My heart wept within me.

I was picked up by another sister from the Bible study class. I spent that night at her house. She had basically told me the same thing, that when I got up in the morning, she would probably be gone to work. Well, when I got up, the telephone rang and I thought it was her calling to check on me. To my surprise, it was my husband. He had found my phone book. Her last name happened to be Anderson. She was the first one he called. He explained that the kids had to get their pictures taken at the school, and the girls needed to get their hair done. Once again, I had to go home. When my friend came home from work, I explained that I was going home and asked if she would take me. She gave me some food to take home. I was so glad to see my children, and they were glad to see me. I wasn't sure what they had thought or felt through this whole ordeal.

For the first time, I saw that my husband showed some kind of concern and looked sorry. After we put the kids to bed, we stayed up and talked. He asked me if I had called my parents and told them that I wanted to come home. Because of the fear, I said, "No, you call them." To God be the glory, he did! He would always call my mother and tell her when he didn't know where I was. My poor mom, but I thanked God for her prayers. I know prayer works, and I'm so thankful! He got on the phone that night, called my parents, and told them that it was time for me to come home. My parents sent me and the children bus tickets. We got the tickets two to three days before we were scheduled to leave.

CHAPTER 7

FREE AT LAST

The day came when we left San Diego, on November 1, 1979, which was my youngest daughter's third birthday. My husband drove us to the bus station. He cried as we got onto the bus. I watched as he drove off as we started to leave San Diego on that Greyhound bus. All praise went to God! He delivered us out of that situation. All glory and praise to His Holy Name. "Call on the Lord and He will show you great and mighty things," (Jer. 33:3). God truly showed me that He was "the Way, the Truth, and the Life," (John 14:6).

The bus ride wasn't that bad with four children. We sat in the back of the bus, so we could be near the bathroom. My son, Charles Jr., made friends with an Indian guy who seemed to be drunk all the time, but friendly. It took us three days to get to Providence, R.I. The Greyhound bus made many stops; it stopped for other people's destinations, pit stops, to change drivers, and to clean the bus. I wasn't sure who picked us up at the Greyhound station. I do remember seeing my mother's face when she first laid eyes on me. It was a sign of terror and relief. We cried as we hugged. It was so good to be home again!

Charles called to make sure we had made it home okay. Back in the day, we didn't have cellphones, so it was a good three days before we spoke again. He was so sad, still crying. He apologized, but knew it was the best thing for me and the kids to be at home with my family.

My children were spoiled with gifts. They received winter clothing, since it was winter there. They were not used to the cold weather. My aunt, who brought them their first snow suits, was the aunt that said my marriage wouldn't last. Maybe she felt guilty, I was not sure. I guessed she was right!

My New Life

I started going back to my old church, Ebernezer Baptist church, with my younger sister, Debbie. We even joined the choir again. We met the church secretary, Shirley O., who was also in the choir. We became friends.

I'm amazed, even to this day, how God puts the right people in our path, at the right time. We were all looking for more of God. We had such a hunger for the things of God. One day, Sister O. saw a flyer that came in the church mail, which was in the trash can. She took it out and saw it was about a "Soul Winner Institute" class that was going to take place at another church. The name of the church was Pentecostal Church of God in Christ at 25 Mystic Street, Providence, R.I. We went to check it out and signed up.

We were not sure what we had gotten ourselves into. It ended up being exactly what we were looking for. We held hands in a circle while we prayed. The presence of the Holy Spirit came into the room. We knew we were missing the Holy Spirit in our lives. The Baptist church didn't teach or even believe in the Holy Spirit. The pastor of the Pentecostal C.O.G.I.C. church was Nathaniel B. Witcher, who opened the doors for the class. He had just come off a forty-day fast.

CHAPTER 8

THE SOUL WINNER'S CLASS

The Soul Winner's Institute class was headed by Sister LaVerne Jackson. She was, and still is, a powerful fireball for God. The classes were taught by her, along with five to six other teachers. We had to really study and learn the Scriptures verbatim. We were taught the proper way to minister the Word to the lost. We were taught how to be compassionate and sensitive to the needs of others, to have a listening ear, to pray with them for their needs, their hurts, and sicknesses, and we even learned how to lead people to the Lord. That was a great feeling inside. People were, and are to this day, hungry for the truth. We learned that not everyone was ready to hear and/or receive the Word. We were told to pray before entering a home. We were always meant to go out with at least two people, but three was even better. There should always be a man with a woman. One of the classes was on the baptism of the Holy Spirit. After learning about the Holy Spirit, we started seeking Him in our lives. We would study the Word at my apartment, night after night. My sister, Debbie, and Sister Shirley, would stay up late. I couldn't hang any later than 10:30 p.m. or 11 p.m. I would fall asleep on the couch, kind of listening to them.

One night, we went to hear a prophet who came to town. We were still seeking the Holy Spirit, and we went, expecting to receive. I got in the line for prayer. I was baptized with the Holy Spirit when I was prayed for, with hands layed on me. I started speaking in tongues, and dancing like I was on cloud nine. It was so awesome! I think we all received the Holy Spirit that night, with the evidence of speaking in tongues.

Sister LaVerne J. really drilled those scriptures into us. I believe the class was sixteen weeks; it was some very intense training.

We then went on a seven-day fast. We were only allowed water, 100% juices, and sugarless mints. During the fast, I was able to cook for the kids without wanting to eat it. The devil was mad. He showed up in many ways.

One day, we noticed there were a lot of flies coming into my apartment. We couldn't tell where they were coming from. I always kept a clean apartment. I never had dirty dishes. The trash was always put outside the house in the dumpster. We even sprayed the kitchen, where they seemed to be. Before we knew it, there were maggots on the kitchen floor. In one of our classes, we learned how the enemy creeps in all kinds of ways. We also learned how to bind and rebuke him. We commanded the devil to flee from my apartment and to never return, in Jesus's Name. It worked! The bugs were gone, praise God. The next thing that happened, there was water coming from the ceiling out of the light bulb fixture. We had to get the maintenance man to come check things out. The family that lived upstairs had run the bathtub over and the water was leaking down. We let Satan know that, *"No weapon formed against us would prosper..."* (Isa. 54:17a). We knew the enemy was mad; people were getting saved. My sister and I even witnessed to our parents. I remember we explained about tithing to my father, who couldn't understand it at first, but when he got it, he got. My dad actually left his church. His mother, brothers, and cousins were still there. My parents both became members of Pentecostal C.O.G.I.C. They also took the Soul Winner's class. Look at God! My dad witnessed to his family. They were upset at first, but eventually, they all came to visit his new church.

At the end of our Soul Winner's class, we had a graduation ceremony and received certificates. We invited family members. We gave our testimonies. I spoke about my separation from Charles, and how I still believed God was going to save him, and put us back together. I know you are probably saying, "*What?*" Right? Well, let me explain. One day, I asked God if Charles would get saved and if we would get back together. Why? Why would I even care about Charles? Well, I knew that Charles was a good person on the inside. He was damaged at a young age from all that he witnessed in Vietnam, as were so many other men and women who made it out of the Vietnam war (or any war for that matter). Charles had shared with me that he went into the tent to get more ammunition and another soldier came in and said, "My turn." He then went out and got blown up. It could have been Charles, but to see that, I couldn't even imagine. God spared Charles's life.

Unfortunately, between that and seeing dead bodies, even children's, it messed him up. The sad part about it is that he never received counselling after coming back to the States. I have written about the bad times between us, but I do remember things about him that I liked. I knew on the inside he could have been a good person, a different person, "if only" he would have let the Lord in. God could have changed him. I sure couldn't! The Bible says, "*All have sinned and come short of the glory of God,*" (Rom. 3:23) I was a sinner saved by grace (Ephesians 2:8). What about you? I asked the Lord if He would save Charles and if we would get back together. One afternoon, I was sitting in the parking lot in my car, waiting for my baby girl, Roxanne, to get out of her Pre-K class. I asked God for a sign (like Gideon). I asked God to show me a dove. The sky was blue, with puffy white clouds. As soon as I had asked, I saw a figure of a dove in the clouds. Then, I asked Him to show me another dove, and before I knew it, they were showing up everywhere. I saw one in the picture on the bedroom wall. I noticed that we used Dove bath soap, and Dove dish detergent. Coincidence or not? *Jesus said, if we ask anything in His name, believe and don't doubt, we shall have it,* " (Mk 11:22-25). I believed! I had faith!

After attending a second Soul Winner's class, Sister LaVerne wanted me to teach a class. She taught me how to present the Soul Winner's class in a nutshell. I really didn't feel as though I was the one to teach the class, but she saw something in me that I didn't see. I sure didn't think that I was capable of teaching the class. With the help of God, I taught the class at Christ Temple church in Providence, R.I. I had about –six to eight students in the class. Sure enough, the students learned how to go out and witness to others. What a great feeling it was to know that I had something to do with souls being saved, through my teaching.

One of my students was my cousin, Sandra Williams. My sister, Debbie, and I witnessed to her when she was in the hospital for an issue with her blood. We shared with her how Jesus had healed the lady in the Bible who had the issue of blood, and how Jesus died so that we might have life and live eternally. We prayed for my cousin's healing and lead her through the Sinner's Prayer. To this day, I believe that she was instantly healed, along with her salvation on that day. She truly confessed, with her mouth, to the Lord Jesus and believed in her heart that Jesus died and rose from the dead to save her. She was truly on fire for the Lord after that day. God used her mightily. She got acquainted with the Apostolic church. She started ministering in Rhode Island, Georgia, Tennessee, Chicago, and Indiana. I believe most of her time was in Chicago, where she worked in the south end side. She counselled men in a drug addiction home. I have a VHS video of her preaching in church. She was laying hands on the sick, prophesying, and people were falling out in the Spirit. She was a powerful woman of God. Unfortunately, Sandra passed away in Florida in 2013 from brain cancer. She was sent to Florida to minister to and receive insight from the Messianic Jews. I didn't understand and will never know why God took her that way. What I do know is that she is in the presence of the Lord. Her preaching/teaching was not in vain. I'm sure she will have one of the most beautiful crowns that was laid up for her in glory. R.I.P Sandra! I love and miss you!

CHAPTER 9
THE VISIT

One day, I got a telephone call from my husband. He wanted to come visit. I agreed to the visit. I had a dream before he came. I saw a figure who seemed to be Jesus, sitting at the foot of my bed. He said to me, "My feet are sweet." I wasn't sure if I mentioned it to Debbie or Sister Shirley or not. I had no idea what that meant, and did not try to find out either. Then I had another dream of a deck of cards. Again, I had no idea what that meant. I kind of thought that that meant some kind of confusion. My husband came. He wanted to give me a ring, but I wouldn't receive it. I wasn't sure if he had brought it for someone else, or if he may have even stolen it. I let my oldest daughter have it. I can't remember how long he stayed, but I was glad when his visit was over. I knew within my spirit that it wasn't time yet. He wasn't saved yet, and still had his worldly ways. He never hit me or anything; we may have argued a few times. I didn't feel in my spirit that it was time for us to re-unite. He did attend church services with me at Pentecostal C.O.G.I.C., and I remember him being prayed over. After he left, I continued to pray for him and continued to believe God.

Pastor Witcher asked me if I was sure I wanted to wait for him, because there were guys in the church that were interested in me. I was sure that God was going to bring my husband back into the picture. The mother of the church, Mother Graves, made sure women were dressed holy. We had to wear dresses below our knees, no pants, no make-up or jewelry, and we had to wear stockings with our high heels or sandals. I enjoyed the teachings in the church. Pastor Witcher was a teacher from his heart. He held revivals and all-night prayer times. My children used to fall asleep on and under the benches. Oh yeah, they got the Word of God in them. The Word would go forth, and the prayers at times were soft, but every three hours it got loud with prayer, praise, songs, clapping, shouting, and speaking in tongues. What a Hallelujah time we had back in the day! During revivals, we would have different speakers. I remember one evangelist who came, and he prayed for my ears. I used to get bad ear infections, and at that time, I had an inner and outer ear infection. He was led by the Spirit of God, and asked who was having problems with their ears. I raised my hand; he came over and laid his hands on my ears, and prayed for me. I was instantly healed. He also prayed for my hands. My hands would literally turn white and purple after coming out of cold weather. When that evangelist prayed for my hands, he said I would lay hands on the sick and they would recover.

My mother was a daycare provider. The great grandmother of two of the children who she cared for was in the hospital. My sister, Debbie, and I went to visit her. The doctors were concerned because she had become jaundiced; her eyes were literally yellow. Debbie and I prayed for her; we laid hands on her, and shortly after, she was discharged from the hospital. Then there was my cousin Sandra, who I already mentioned. She was healed after my sister, Debbie, and I prayed and laid our hands on her.

CHAPTER 10

THE CHRISTMAS MIRACLE

S ister Shirley had purchased a house. She lived on the first floor and I lived on the second floor. Our children attended a Christian school. Their school was in Barrington, R.I. One morning, we got ready to take them to school, and the car wouldn't start. The school was about a forty-five to fifty minute drive. We laid hands on that car and prayed. Thank God, it started! Hallelujah! All praise was given to God. He always made ways out of no ways. Another time He came through for us was during Christmas. We had already both brought Christmas trees and decorated them. Christmas was quickly approaching. Sister Shirley and I were struggling financially. We didn't know how we were going to get the children gifts. One afternoon, I received a phone call; the person on the other end said that she was calling from Santa's center. I didn't believe in Santa, but I listened to what she had to say. She asked if Ms. Shirley and myself would be home to receive a package. I immediately said, "yes." When Sister Shirley came home from work, I told her about the phone call. We fed the kids and let them play upstairs while we waited downstairs. We were so excited, not knowing what it could be. We were guessing that maybe it was a car, or this or that, or maybe toys for the kids.

Finally, the doorbell rang, and the person outside the door asked if I lived upstairs or downstairs. I said, "upstairs." I was asked to go and open my front door. Oh my, I thought! Sister Shirley and I looked at each other. I ran up the back stairs, down the front stairs, and opened the door. As I opened my door, I saw someone going into Sister Shirley's door, holding what looked like a lady's coat on a coat hanger. Someone was also coming into my door, and I brought them upstairs. Before I knew it, people kept coming in with things in their hands.

When they were finished, Sister Shirley came upstairs with the people who had delivered the gifts. They wanted to pray with all of us. We got the children from the bedroom, and we all held hands in a circle. I believe there were at least six or seven of them who delivered the gifts. The man who prayed for us, I cannot remember what he had said, but I remember that he went into his inside coat pocket and pulled out two envelopes. He gave one to Sister Shirley and one to me. What a miracle that took place that night. He told us that the gifts were from God. We were in awe and thanked them all. Sister Shirley and I walked them to the door, as we continued to thank them. We believed that they were angels sent by God. We didn't see anything but a pickup truck. It was really a cold night. Sister Shirley and I went back upstairs with the kids. We couldn't believe our eyes the Christmas tree had so many gifts under it. We opened the envelopes. Inside the envelopes, there were $50 for each child and $50 for ourselves.

All we could do was praise the Lord, for blessing us abundantly. As we looked at the gifts under the tree, we were in awe; the gift tags for the kids had their names on them, and read, "From Jesus!" They received clothes, socks, PJ's, sweaters, gloves, hats, toys, and so much more. There was also food, a meal for Christmas, detergent, etc. Sister Shirley and I also received coats, ones that accurately fit us! Glory to God in the highest. What a Christmas miracle it was! It was exceedingly, abundantly above all we could ever ask or think (Eph. 3:20). The next night, we went to church with our new coats and clothes on, and testified of what the Lord had done. God showed up and showed out! (Jer. 33:3).

CHAPTER 11

THE EVANGELIST FROM ATLANTA, GEORGIA

One Friday night, Pastor Nathaniel Witcher wanted the members to go visit another church; they were having an evangelist from out of town that night. The evangelist was from Atlanta, Georgia. I cannot remember the message given, but I went up for prayer. As I was waiting to be prayed for, one of the women who came with the evangelist from Atlanta came up to me and spoke with me. She took two bracelets off her arm and placed them on my arm. I sure wish I could remember what she told me at that time. I felt the presence of God even more. The evangelist came to me, but before he prayed for me, he prophesied over Roxanne (her second prophecy) and over her life. He told me that she had a double anointing over her life. The first time was when we had first gotten to Rhode Island.

The reason I went up for prayer this night was because I had heard from Charles. He had called me and told me that he got saved. I had told him that I wasn't coming back to California. I also told him that we should pray about it and ask God what we should do. I really don't know why I said that, knowing I didn't want to go back to California, and be 3,000 miles away from my family again. After the evangelist prayed for me, I went out in the Spirit. When I got up, I knew, I really knew, that I was going back to California. I was so sure of myself that I told everyone even before we left that church, that I was going back to California. Of course, everyone was shocked, as you readers probably are!

Back to San Diego

The day came when the children and I were getting back on the Greyhound bus, and headed to San Diego. They were crying. I knew that they were sad to leave their friends and family members, and I was sure that they were probably afraid of the thought of going back to live with their dad.

Once back in San Diego, Charles picked us up at the Greyhound station. I shortly realized that we didn't have a place to live. We ended up driving around looking for an apartment. Charles went into places and got applications. When it started getting dark, we ended up staying at a hotel. The next morning, I was still very tired. We ate breakfast and I told Charles to take Charles Jr. and go look for an apartment, and the girls and I would stay and rest at the hotel. He agreed. Before they left, I felt lead to pray for them before they went out looking. They were out for only a half hour, when Charles called the hotel room and said that they found a place for us to move in. He said that the landlord's husband and wife were saved. Look at God!

I knew this was a big step of faith my coming back to San Diego. We moved into our apartment up at the top of a hill, on the second floor. Charles had some furniture, but not much. God met our needs: "Jehovah Jireh," our Provider. Within a week or two, we had all that we needed. God was really a Miracle Worker, since neither one of us had a job. Charles shared his testimony with the landlords when he had first met them, even though he didn't realize it was a testimony. Praise the Lord! We ended up visiting the church of the landlords. That church became our church home. We fell in love with the pastor, his wife, the congregation, and vice versa. It so happened that our anniversary was the same as Pastor and First Lady Anderson: not only the same day, but the month and year, what a coincidence. Charles and I shared our testimonies and that become our church home.

I remember our first Thanksgiving; we were blessed with so much food. Our cupboards literally were running over. We were blessed to be a blessing. We shared food with our neighbors.

Charles ended up getting a job with one of the brothers of the church. He became an insurance agent. Thank the Lord for a job. The rent would get paid. Things went well for a while, but before long, Charles's job kept him out longer than he probably needed to be. A trick of the enemy. His job seemed to be taking him to females' homes, which was one of his weaknesses in our marriage. He started being too tired to go to church on Sundays. Before I knew it, he had no desire to go at all. Pastor Anderson and Brother Carl (the guy that got him the job) would call and even come visit him. Finally, he started going back to church. On Sunday evenings, we would watch Jimmy Swaggart Ministries. Charles found out that Jimmy Swaggart had a college. He became interested in going. He sent for and received an application. He filled it out, mailed it, and was accepted.

He told our pastor that he was accepted into the college and that we would be moving to Louisiana to attend the college. The church family was sad to see us leave. They gave us a going-away party before we left. We were financially able to make the trip to Louisiana. I mentioned earlier is this book that Charles's hometown was in Louisiana. When we left, we left with suitcases only, and drove to Louisiana. I wasn't sure of what car we drove, but it broke down in Louisiana before we reached the college. We ended up at his parent's house. Charles had said that he was expecting to receive his last check from the insurance company, along with his commission. We ended up staying at his parent's house, week after week. I wasn't even sure how long. The house was crowded already. There were a total of fifteen people, including his parents and the six of us. I learned that he didn't come from a loving home; there was so much hatred. I felt as though I could cut it with a knife. There was a lot of arguing. Oh, how we wished his check would come, so the car could get fixed and we could get to the college. I had decided to fast for a day or two. His mother thought I was out of my mind. She thought it was evil to fast. We explained that it was biblical. I thanked God for Sunday. Everyone in the house went to church, except their father. He mostly stayed to himself. He would sit on the back porch, smoking cigarettes and drinking his black coffee. I'm not sure if it was mixed with alcohol or not .

CHAPTER 12

PRAYER AND FASTING WORKS

efore the service started, we heard people behind us talking. The older woman was introducing her niece who had just come from California. We also heard that the niece was a member of a full gospel church. When Charles and I had heard that, we made sure we spoke to them after the church service. I knew it was God who had us speak to them. We shared that we had come from San Diego, California ourselves. Charles shared the story of how we were supposed to be going to J.S.B.C., and our dilemma. The aunt told us that she has prayer every morning at 6 a.m., if we were interested. We sure were interested, but couldn't get there, because we didn't have a car. Charles asked his mother if he could use her car, but she wouldn't let him. She didn't believe in all that praying in the morning stuff. One day, we got a ride to the aunt's house; we were told to call her Aunt Bea. Aunt Bea had a four or five-bedroom house and plenty of land. I was not sure how we got there that morning, but were welcomed to come stay at her house, until his check came. Look at how He answered our prayer! We packed up our clothing and moved into Aunt Bea's place.

Our time there was like heaven on earth. The kids were able to play and have fun, probably like never before. They would help Aunt Bea in her garden, picking beans, corn, okra, etc. Yes, we had fresh food right from the garden. We would get up in the morning for our six o'clock prayer and then Aunt Bea would cook us breakfast. Oh, that down south bacon, home fries, scrambled eggs, and homemade biscuits, not to forget the homemade jam! Oh, the joy!

One day Charles's family called Aunt Bea's house. His mother also knew Aunt Bea; they may even have been distant cousins. The person who called said that my parents had called there looking for us, and I needed to give them a call. My parents knew Charles's parents' number, because I had called them when we had first arrived in Louisiana, and I had explained our situation with the car and check. Remember, there were no cellphones back then, only home phones and a thing called long distance. I asked Aunt Bea if I could call home, and she said yes. God was still at work. I called and explained where and why we were staying at Aunt Bea's house. They told me to ask Aunt Bea if they could come. They were on their way to San Antonio, TX, to go visit my brother and his family. They wanted to make a stop in Louisiana to see us. Aunt Bea was delighted and said, "Yes, that would be great."

My parents arrived in the wee hours of the morning; they came by Greyhound bus. Charles and I went to pick them up in Aunt Bea's car. My parents were dropped off on the side of the road, not sure how they even were able to call us. When we first spotted them, they were sitting on their suitcases, by the side of the road. Thank God that He watched over them. Aunt Bea was up when we got back. We talked for a short while, then she showed them where they would spend the night. She also told them about the six o'clock prayer session, but I was not sure if we made that one.

The next morning, when we all got up, breakfast was ready and smelling so good. My parents were so grateful for Aunt Bea. My dad, of course, wanted to pay her for our stay, but she refused any money. It was nice to see my parents again; it had been about a year since the kids and I had seen them. Aunt Bea invited my parents to stay and go on a fast with her; I believed it was a three-day fast. Surprisingly, my parents said yes; well, really my mother talked my father into it. Well, the enemy got mad. The pipes under the house started leaking. My dad and husband did all they could do to fix it, but Aunt Bea had to call for professional help. This was during our fasting time, but it didn't disturb our time in the Lord. We had prayer at six a.m., at noon, and at three p.m. What an awesome time, with songs, testimonies, prayer, and more! My father and Charles wanted the baptism in the Holy Spirit, and my mother and I wanted a refilling. It all happened that night. It was an awesome Holy Spirit-filled night. Glory to God!

The time came for my parents to make their way to Texas. The reason they wanted to make the stop in Louisiana was to give us money to get the car fixed. Look at God! We took my parents to the bus station and saw them off.

Remember, I had asked for a sign when I was waiting for my youngest child, Roxanne, to come out of her Pre-K class. I had asked if Charles and I would get back together, and if he would be saved and baptized with the Holy Spirit? Well, he received the baptism of the Holy Spirit that night. Hallelujah!

Charles had missed the enrollment date for the college. With the money my father gave us, Charles was able to get the car fixed. We headed to Rhode Island, where my father told us to go.

CHAPTER 13

DELIVERED

*O*nce back in Rhode Island, we stayed at my parents' home for a short time. God came through again. Charles got a maintenance job at an apartment complex, which allowed us to get a four-bedroom apartment. Look at God! We attended the same church that I left before we moved. I met the lady my dad had told me about when I was in California. He told me that this lady and her daughter had moved from Maryland and joined the church. My dad had said he really thought this lady and I had a lot in common, and that I would like her. After church one Sunday, he invited them over to the house for dinner. He was right, and we became like family. Her daughter was a few years younger than my youngest daughter. We are all friends today! My new friend was going through a marital situation and I was glad I had a listening ear and a mind to pray with and for her. To God be the glory!

As for my marital situation, Charles did good for a while, until he got caught up with drugs and a secretary who seemed to be interested in him, *even* after finding out that I was his wife. She used to be friends with one of my first cousins. As always, he fell for the trick of the enemy. Due to working that job, he didn't get Sundays off. He never got grounded in the Word of God.

Things got so bad that he started stealing things out of the home. I'm not sure what happened to his car. He stole my daughter's bike that she got for christmas and never brought it back. I also worked. One day, when I came home my daughter was so upset that she had a butcher knife. I was not sure what was going on, but I knew it was time to end this mess. I had mentioned it to my parents and my aunt May. Aunt May said she was going to put me in her book (a prayer request). She also told me to read Psalms 91. She said to cover my children, myself, and my home with Psalms 91. In a nutshell, it says God's Angels will watch over us and protect us. We need not fear. Verse 15 says, "When they call on me, I will answer, I will be with them in trouble." God gave me such a peace.

Charles lost his job. He no longer could be trusted. I had decided to move without him. I was now attending Providence Assemble of God church. One Sunday right after church service, Charles wanted to speak to me outside.

I was gripped with fear, but remembered Psalms 91. I went out, not sure what he was saying. Other people were still out there in front of the church. One couple came up to us, after hearing some of our conversation. I'm not sure what they said to us, but I do remember them inviting us to come to their house for dinner. I really believed it was a move of God. They lived about thirty minutes from the church. As we were driving to their home, they were ministering to us. We felt the presence of the Lord in that vehicle. The cassette tape was playing, with Phil Driscoll singing and playing on his horn "You Are Great, You Do Miracles So Great." Between them talking to us and that music, we both were weeping.

We finally arrive at their home. They had a total of ten children, and some of them had stayed home. As the wife was cooking, they still were ministering with us. I supposed I shared some of my concerns. God did it again; He opened up another door for us. They told us that their third floor was available and if we wanted, we could move up there and rent it, so we did.

I was not sure how long that lasted, but it didn't solve Charles's problem. Again, he found the drugs, or the drugs found him. One day, I came home from work and my husband and oldest daughter were literally fighting. Nothing was fixed in our marriage. We even went to counselling with my pastor. He gave Charles a scripture which basically said that the time would come and that it would be too late. I would be gone.

CHAPTER 14

THE LAST STRAW

*W*ell, that time finally came. I was living at another location, but of course had taken him back. The kids were all grown now in their own places. Charles was receiving fifty percent disability from the VA, but applied for one hundred percent. He was told by his friends that he could get one hundred percent if he went in acting crazy. Well for sure, he did just that and he got it. I couldn't see myself working full-time and him getting as much as I got working, not to mention the stress of him begging for the money, as he always did. I had control of his money. So, I started working part-time. I decided to go on vacation for a month; I needed to get away. I went to visit my sister in Atlanta, Georgia. There was a family that was also going to Georgia. I ended up riding with them and helped drive their ten-passenger van. That was a great ride with a loving family, the Jacksons. We went there during the Olympics in 1996. I stayed with my sister for the month. My sister and I did visit downtown and saw some of the Olympic venues. It was nice to get away. I drove back to Rhode Island with the Jackson family.

When I finally picked up by Charles from the Jackson's home, I could tell things were not ever going to be right between us. He dropped me off at home and said he had to go somewhere. I went into the house and found evidence that a female had been in my place. Somehow, I made it to my parents' home and I stayed. I could not bring myself to go back to that place. He threatened me over the phone, and I got a restraining order. One Saturday, my friend Mary came over and told us that Charles was in front of her friend's house. He was in a parked car kissing a young girl who was around the age of my daughters. That was the last straw. I remember my sister and brother-in-law telling me that I was welcome to come back any time. Well, I called and asked them if I could come back and stay until I got a job and my own place; they said yes! I left Rhode Island and all of my belongings again, and moved to Georgia on October 4th, 1996. My middle daughter, Carla, and her two children came with me. We took the train to Georgia.

Was it really the last straw? No. After a few years, Charles ended up in his hometown, where he moved with that young girl. I'm pretty sure too much drugs caught up with him. He ended up having an aneurysm. His children went and visited him in the VA hospital. To make a long story short, he survived that and was put in the VA medical center, where he was cared for by the staff. He and I used to talk over the phone. His daughters visited him and so did I once. He had dedicated his life back to the Lord and was attending church services regularly. He finally realized that he loved me, but as the pastor had warned him, it was too late. He passed away in 2019 with kidney failure. I thanked God that he found out Jesus loved him through it all and that Jesus died for him, and he now has eternal life with the Father. To God be the glory!

CHAPTER 15

RIGHTEOUS LIVING

*I*n order to be delivered, we have to totally surrender ourselves to God, or we will continue to go in circles, as the Israelites did. To surrender, one has to die to self (the flesh) and let the Spirit of God have complete control. *"For all have sinned and fall short of the glory of God,"* *(Rom. 3:23)* It is God's grace and mercy that sets us free from Satan's trap. *"For God so loved the world, that He gave His only begotten Son, that whoever believes in Him should not perish but have eternal life," (John 3:16). "For whoever calls on the name of the Lord shall be saved," (Rom. 10:13) "That if you confess with your mouth the Lord Jesus and believe in your heart that God has raised Jesus from the dead, you will be saved. For with the heart one believes unto righteousness, and with the mouth confession is made unto salvation," (Rom. 10:9-10).*

In the book of Romans 8, it talks about living free from sin:

> *There is therefore now no condemnation to those who are in Christ Jesus, who do not walk according to the flesh, but according to the Spirit. For the law of the Spirit of life in Christ Jesus, has made me free from the spirit of sin and death. For what the law could not do in that it was weak through the flesh, God did by sending His own Son in the likeness of sinful flesh, on account of sin: He condemned sin*

*in the flesh, that the righteous requirement of the law might
be fulfilled in us who do not walk according to the flesh but
according to the Spirit. For those who live according to the
flesh set their minds on things of the flesh, but those who
live according to the Spirit the things of the Spirit. For to
be carnally minded is death, but to be spiritually minded is
life and peace. Because the carnal mind is enmity against
God; for it is not subject to the law of God, nor indeed can
be. So then, those who are in the flesh cannot please God.*
Romans 8:1–8

The book of Romans has so much to offer as to how we should live
a righteous life before God. I truly recommend reading it for all. *"And
we know that all things work together for good to those who love God, to
those who are the called according to His purpose," (Rom. 8:28).*

THE LORD'S PRAYER

Our Father in heaven, Hallowed be Your name. Your kingdom come. Your will be done on earth as it is in heaven. Give us this day our daily bread. And forgive us our debts, as we forgive our debtors. And do not lead us into temptation, but deliver us from the evil one. For Yours is the Kingdom and the power and the glory forever, Amen. Matthew 6:1-13

Prayer of Salvation

Father God, Your Word says, "That whosoever calls on the name of the Lord shall be saved." Today, I call on the name of the Lord Jesus. I believe that Jesus came and gave His life on Calvary for me. I believe that He died on the cross, that He was buried, and that He rose from the dead. I also believe that He is alive and is seated with You in Heaven. I ask Jesus to forgive me of my sins, and to come into my heart and make me new.

ABOUT THE AUTHOR

*L*oretta Thomas is a woman of faith. She was born and raised in Providence, Rhode Island. She got saved at the age of twelve. At the age of eighteen, she fell into Satan's trap.

She is blessed with four children, fourteen grandchildren, and eight great grandchildren, with the youngest great grandchild born in December of 2021.

Loretta survived domestic violence. She married a Marine, who had served in the Vietnam War, and suffered from Post-Traumatic Stress Disorder. The only way he knew how to cope was with drugs and women.

Loretta was trapped, living in San Diego 3,000 miles away from her family. One night, she almost lost her life after filing for a divorce. It was a living nightmare, and a night she will never forget: October 22, 1979. On November 1, 1979, she left San Diego and her husband behind. Due to her faith, they reunited in 1984. The last straw came in 1996. Loretta is now single and has never remarried or dated. Her love for the Lord has kept her.

Loretta is a volunteer at Living Well Adult Daycare in McDonough, GA. She is a member of Tabernacle of Praise Church International, with Pastor T.J. and First Lady Shunnae' McBride.

CPSIA information can be obtained
at www.ICGtesting.com
Printed in the USA
BVHW031112260722
643032BV00015B/840